Careers to Explore: Brownie and Junior Leaders' Guide

Girl Scouts of the U.S.A.
830 Third Avenue
New York, N.Y. 10022

Inquiries related to *Careers to Explore:
Brownie and Junior Leaders' Guide*
should be addressed to the Program
Department, Girl Scouts of the U.S.A., 830
Third Avenue, New York, N.Y. 10022.

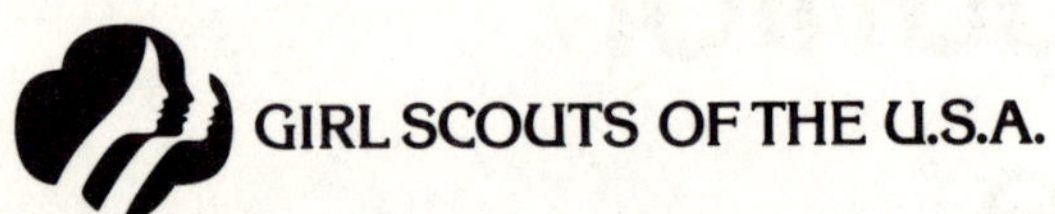 GIRL SCOUTS OF THE U.S.A.

Mrs. Orville L. Freeman, *President*
Frances R. Hesselbein, *National
Executive Director*

Copyright © 1979 by Girl Scouts of the United States of America
All rights reserved
First Impression 1979, Third Printing October 1980
Printed in the United States of America
Girl Scout Catalog No. 20-814-000
ISBN 0-88441-325-X

Contents

What Is *Careers to Explore*?

Careers to Explore for Brownie and Junior Girl Scouts is an introduction to career exploration. It is designed for Juniors and older Brownies. It includes an activity and interview book for girls and this leaders' guide.

As you will see, the girls' book includes activity ideas and interviews with women in a wide assortment of careers. The book is divided into the five worlds of Girl Scout program to encourage the use of this material with *Worlds to Explore: Handbook for Brownie and Junior Girl Scouts*. There is also an introductory section, called "All About Careers," devoted to careers in general, which has additional activity ideas and interviews. Each activity is divided into four sections as follows:

The opening paragraph serves as an introduction to the activity and seeks to relate the experiences of girls to the particular topic.

The following material encourages girls to observe things that they may have overlooked in their daily lives, and to enhance their involvement with community and family.

The next section directly involves girls in a project. They might design a book, print a picture, or conduct an interview. This part of the activity helps build upon the framework of observation and introspection to provide an active learning experience.

Additional suggestions allow girls who are interested in a particular topic to go on with further exploration. Some girls will choose not to continue working on a project after their initial explorations. This is acceptable because the additional suggestions are optional.

Questions about Career Exploration

Why is career exploration part of the Girl Scout program?

Career exploration materials were developed by GSUSA to help young girls become aware of the many opportunities that will be open to them in the future and to begin preparing them for those opportunities. The activities and interviews in the girls' book will encourage them to:

- examine their values, interests, and activities,
- explore a wide assortment of careers within their community and elsewhere,
- consider future career possibilities for themselves,
- develop positive attitudes towards career choices for women.

How does Careers to Explore *fit into ongoing Girl Scout program?*

Careers to Explore is a supplement to other Girl Scout program materials. It offers you and the girls additional activity ideas which can be used individually, as part of a special careers project, or in conjunction with other troop activities, such as work on Brownie B activities, badges, or signs.

The activities are designed for use by either large or small groups. Many activities can also be done by girls on their own, although sharing ideas at a later time is always a good idea. All activities are designed to be done in any order the girls and you choose, although it is suggested that the section called "All About Careers" might be an appropriate starting point.

Can I use Careers to Explore *with the girls, even though I don't know a lot about different careers?*

Yes. You bring girls your personal enthusiasm and your knowledge of how to find new information. You explore careers together with them and share the learning experience.

During a lifetime, everyone makes many career decisions. Some decisions involve paid employment, others do not. You can help girls understand that career choices such as volunteer work, homemaking, or parenthood are as valuable and important as a business or professional career.

Community business representatives can be asked to work with your troop. Your personal friends and neighbors who may be involved in various careers can be another source of help. By arranging for trips and speakers, you will be able to help girls learn about the world of working women.

Why do young girls and women need to explore career opportunities?

Almost every magazine for women today has at least one article on careers. This has happened because women are entering and reentering the work force in unexpected numbers. As they do, they want to know how to plan a career that meets their needs and will provide for long-term satisfaction. Many of the following factors have brought about this increase of women entering the work force.

Economic Factors. More women need to be self-supporting or to help with family finances.

Physical Factors. Women have a longer life span, thereby increasing the years they can devote to a career.

Educational Factors. Women are entering higher education and training programs in increasing numbers. Learning is a lifelong process in today's rapidly changing world. Educational opportunities in nontraditional career areas for women are increasing.

Social Factors. Many social factors have created a positive climate toward working women. Thus, barriers to women in careers (particularly high-paying and/or nontraditional careers) are slowly breaking down.

Distinctions between male and female roles are being reexamined in today's society.

Single parent homes are increasing and many single parents need jobs.

Families are smaller and parents have more time and energy for employment.

Exposure to more and varied female role models motivates young women to prepare actively for their futures.

How do the behavioral differences between boys and girls affect their view of career choices?

Many behavioral differences between the sexes are based on what society has said girls *ought* to do or boys *ought* to do. Because of this, girls have tended to have less confidence than boys in their ability to assert themselves, plan their lives, and control their futures. Many girls have been encouraged to be passive and to avoid risks and competition. This in turn limits their ideas of career choices.

For today's girls, all choices should be open. Girls should be encouraged in developing prosocial behaviors—the nurturing capacities such as caring, sharing, and loving as well as the assertive capacities such as getting things done. Ideally, men and women can learn to share both the nurturing roles and the assertive roles.

How can I help the girls in my group to believe in themselves?

By working with young girls and seeing how *Careers to Explore* fits your group's interests, you've taken the first step. Here are other ways to help.

Accept the fact that differences exist among girls, but realize that these differences lend richness to life and to your group. Create a climate of caring and support for each girl. Through the use of role models in the interviews, show group members that you appreciate the diversity among peoples.

Believe that girls should reach their full potential as human beings and help them expand their knowledge and skills. All girls have different levels of ability depending upon their age, physical development, life experiences, and the task before them. Girls need practice in discovering their special skills and in learning that individually and as a group they have a wealth of abilities to bring to any task (and any career).

Girls need practice, too, in making decisions and taking responsibility for their decisions. As girls practice making decisions (even though they may make mistakes), they gain the skills for making responsible decisions in the future.

How to Use *Careers to Explore* with Girls

You should become familiar with the activities and the interviews before attempting to share them with the girls. Then, at a troop meeting, allow the girls to become acquainted with the materials. Give them time to look at the activities and allow them to observe the pictures. They might like to look at all the interviews and share their interests and ideas in the Brownie Ring or Junior patrol groups.

At the next meeting, girls can browse through the pages again to refresh their memories and to find their favorite activities and interviews. At that point, when girls feel totally comfortable, allow them to select activities that interest them.

An alternative approach is to work through the materials, world by world, letting the group decide which world they will explore at each week's meeting.

Still another approach would be to choose activities in one world each week, followed by interviews in that same world the following week. That way, you can continue with one particular area of interest for a longer time.

You and your troop may discover other ways of using these materials. There are no right or wrong ways to use them. The activities are designed to make career education enjoyable. If girls choose activities they like and are interested in, then they will become involved and profit from using the materials. By all means, follow your own ideas. Only you know which format will work best with your troop.

Here are some more ways to help girls gain an awareness of careers through these materials.

Discussion Sessions

Many girls will have questions about the activities and interviews. Encourage open sharing experiences in the troop to help answer these questions. As girls acquire information on different careers, they will become more excited about and interested in asking questions and in sharing what they know.

The girls may question why they do not know any "real life" women in the careers featured in the interviews and activities. It is important to explain that this may be true, but more and more women every day are going into new and different types of work. Girls who are very young now will have even more opportunities in their futures.

Some girls may question whether a woman can handle a career and a family. Or they may be skeptical about women doing jobs where traditionally only men were involved. Use these issues, discuss and debate them. Ask the girls how they might work out such problems in their own lives. Give them the time to think through these questions. Have girls share their solutions to problems. Use the interviews to show how many of the career women have solved similar problems.

Independent Research

If a girl has enjoyed a particular activity, she might want to follow up on her own. Encourage girls to become involved by asking questions about careers of people in their own families or of adult friends. These adults are extremely good resources for heightening career awareness in young children. Encourage girls to be aware of women's roles in their reading at home, in school, and at the library.

Art and Writing Materials

A number of activities involve making things. The materials needed for these activities should be gathered before troop meeting time. Especially with Brownies, it's a good idea to have all materials set up and ready to use. Leaders are encouraged to allow adequate planning time for troop meetings, thereby being able to anticipate which materials will be needed.

Many of the activities in these materials call for written expression. These can still be accomplished by girls who do not yet read or write well. Have them tell you what they would like to write and then have them draw their observations. This method encourages girls to want to read their own stories.

Trips and Speakers

The business world is a very important part of career education and awareness. Use it as a resource. There are probably many work sites in your own community to visit and many career women who might be willing to speak at your troop meeting. These women can tell about the work they do and answer questions for the girls. There may even be women with unusual careers in your own community that are not represented by the interviews in the book. They, too, can help broaden the girls' awareness of careers.

It is fun to plan trips to job sites to meet with workers and discover what happens there. To plan a trip, it is important to keep these points in mind:

- Obtain written permission from parents and from your local council, as well as permission from the job site the girls will visit.
- Invite other adults along to help supervise the trip.
- Before the trip, prepare the girls about where they will go and what they will see. Have a preliminary discussion about the site, the workers, and your expectations of the girls' behavior while there.

Follow up the trip by having each girl discuss her reactions. Is she interested in working in any of the careers she saw? Why or why not?

Have the girls send a thank-you note to the people at the job site. Besides being courteous, it helps keep the door open for other Girl Scout troops in your community to enjoy similar visits.

Community Resources

Local resources include businesses, schools, the local library, museums, the Chamber of Commerce, women's and men's groups, professional organizations, government agencies, and local newspaper editors. Many would probably be delighted to help girls expand their career horizons. In many instances, these same resources exist on a national level. There are also many books, pamphlets, filmstrips, and other materials available in career education. Use your local library if you wish to locate these and perhaps expand on some of the ideas in the activities.

Interview Activities

The following activities are designed to generate interest in the careers featured in the interviews.

Once they are familiar with all of the interviews, girls may wish to make a deck of career interview "playing" cards. Label each card to match one of the interviews in the girls' book. Begin by dealing out a hand of interview cards to each girl, one at a time, until the entire stack of cards has been dealt out. Then, do any of the following activities.

Have each girl describe the place where a person would work for the career shown on a card in her hand. Each time a troop member describes a similar work site from a card in her hand, have her place her card on top of those cards for the same place of work. At the end of the game, talk about the careers in each of these stacks.

Have girls choose a troop member whom they think would be a good person for the career shown on one card. Ask the girl to guess what talent or personality trait she has that prompted her to be chosen for that career.

Have each girl list the careers on the cards she is holding and write down the subjects studied in school that might help in each of these careers. Have each girl read her list. Talk about it. Which school subjects were mentioned most often? Which careers require skills that are not taught as subjects in school?

Play Career Charades. Have each girl act out one of the careers in her hand. Have the other players guess the career.

Suggest that half the girls choose a card and join with another person to act out a short skit in which they meet and describe their careers to each other. Or act out a humor-ous episode involving the roles of the career persons on your cards.

Have ready a stack of sheets of heavy wrapping paper, crayons, large blunt-edged needles, scissors, and balls of heavy string or yarn. Have each player choose a card from her hand and make a costume or uniform to be worn at work in that career.

Have ready several large sheets of white paper and several boxes of crayons or tempera paints and brushes. When each girl has selected a card from her hand, have the girls join together in small groups to create murals showing the career people at work in one place, such as an office, a resort or park, a medical center. Or have the girls draw a town, showing on-the-job views of the careers. Display the completed mural in a location where others can enjoy it.

Do this orally or on paper. Have one girl select a career card from her hand and begin a story about someone in that career. After one or two paragraphs, pass the story to the left and ask the next person to add the next paragraph. After the story has gone around the table, read it aloud to the group.

Have girls individually list (with leader or girls recording) the careers most interesting to them. Compare the girls' lists.

For more individual activities, distribute one card to each troop member and suggest one of the following:

Act out an imaginary episode a worker might experience while working at that career.

Write a TV or magazine commercial to recruit applicants for the career shown on the card.

Write a short poem or song about the career on a card.

More Activities to Explore Careers

This section will give you additional activity ideas in all five worlds to explore, as well as in the area of careers in general. It is meant to help you expand troop activities beyond the pages of the girls' book, when interest in a particular area is especially high.

The activities are all written "to the girl" so that you can read them directly to your troop, if you'd like. Each activity suggestion will probably trigger you and the girls to think of several additional ones on your own.

For activities involving troop visits, in most cases you will need to make advance arrangements. See *Planning Trips With Girl Scouts* (Cat. No. 19-998) for details on how to do this.

More "All About Careers" Activities

Draw murals depicting various activities and scenes in your future life.

Write "Help Wanted" ads featuring the things you do best.

Find out about projects in your community that require cooperation between many career groups.

Observe people at work in many different settings. Look for patterns of sex, cultural group, and age in workers.

Working involves sharing and getting along with people as well as finishing jobs. Discuss ways to accomplish these tasks.

Choose a product and try to envision its production from beginning to end.

Choose a skill you have and demonstrate it for the troop.

Visit a hardware or office supply store or any store that sells tools and materials used by workers. Talk about the tools you see and how they might be used.

A person may have many careers in a lifetime. Talk about people you know who have changed careers.

Think about and discuss this question: Which is more important, to do something you like or something that pays a lot of money?

Present skits or puppet shows about a career you have discovered.

More "World of Well-Being" Activities

Attend a girls' or women's sports event.

Listen to talking books, look at a book written in Braille, or find out about other aids for people with special needs.

Talk to a veterinarian, blacksmith, horse trainer, pet shop owner, sheepherder, dog groomer, or anyone who works with animals.

Make a list of the paid and unpaid jobs that would be good for someone who likes children.

Visit a community agency or house of worship to find out about some of the services available to families.

Make a floor plan of an imaginary hospital and mark on it where various jobs are done in the hospital.

Talk to someone at a YWCA or neighborhood center to find out about the kinds of instructors they hire and the backgrounds needed.

In the sports pages of a newspaper, follow the events in which women athletes are participating in your area, across the country, or around the world.

Look through the yellow pages of your local telephone directory to find the different health careers pursued in your area.

Talk to someone who cooks or bakes for a living in a restaurant, delicatessen, bakery, hotel, motel, fast food spot, etc. Find out what qualifications are needed for her/his job.

More "World of People" Activities

Discuss the Promise and Law and the meaning of service in Girl Scouting.

Invite a great-grandparent or grandparent to visit the troop and talk about her or his career and how it has changed over the years.

Think about careers that may have been popular at one time but now have disappeared. Talk about why careers change.

Visit a police station to find out about the many careers in law enforcement.

Choose a country to explore, find out how women's and men's roles are defined there. Study the customs and traditions, the geography and climate.

Write to girls in different parts of the world. Here is an organization to help you find pen pals:

> The Big Blue Marble
> Dept. G.S., P.O. Box 4054
> Santa Barbara, Calif. 93103

List careers that you feel are "traditional" roles for women.

Talk about sharing work. Can you see the concept of teamwork being used to help do things in the troop? Make a kaper chart for troop duties.

Make a family tree. Share your family's heritage with other troop members. (For this activity, sensitivity to each girl's situation is imperative.)

Divide into two or more teams and hold a relay race or give a team-planned skit. Talk about the ways you helped each other to make the team work together smoothly.

More "World of Today and Tomorrow" Activities

Visit a freight yard, railroad signal tower or railway station, airport and control tower.

Talk to the people in your local Girl Scout equipment agency about their jobs.

Find out about the process for getting a patent.

Learn about some of the principles of flying, through building a model plane or flying a battery-operated plane.

Design bridges (with an erector set, blocks, or on paper) to suit the following situations:

- a footbridge across a mountain stream that rises many feet when the snow melts in the spring
- a car and bicycle bridge across a wide, quiet lake
- a train bridge across a medium-sized river
- a footbridge across a highway next to an airport
- a bridge for cars and heavy trucks across a large bay

Talk to a painter, plumber, electrician, or other repairperson about her/his work.

Visit a local bank to find out about the services it offers, who helps you with each service, and the work involved.

Visit a power station, a coal mine, an oil refinery, the gas or electric company, to find out about energy production and jobs.

List the jobs that might be done on a new car for your family from the moment it is first assembled until it reaches your home. Ask a new car dealer or garage mechanic for help.

Investigate jobs related to food production: in research labs, on the farm, in storage, in transit, in stores, or in preparation (canned, cooked, frozen, packaged).

Talk to a woman in real estate about the cost of houses and apartments in your area and the changes in the market in recent years.

Design some kind of energy-saving device that could be used on a house, such as a solar water heater or a windmill.

More "World of the Arts" Activities

Print a poster to announce a troop or school project.

Experiment with a design in several colors. First, print background design, then overlay with different colors.

Improvise a dance that might celebrate a wedding, end of a year, or birth of a baby.

Portray different animals through short dances. Imagine different motions the animal would make if confronted by danger, or if caring for its young.

Using a tape recorder, take turns reading, reciting, or making up answers to questions. Play back the recordings and talk about voice sounds, diction, and skills needed by radio announcers.

Talk about famous puppet characters and their personalities. How are they like real people? How are they different?

Bring books, magazines, and newspapers to a troop meeting. Compare photographs, styles of art, and methods of telling stories.

Collect ten pictures (may be actual photos or magazine pictures) which tell about your hobbies, likes, dislikes, favorite clothing, etc.

Teach songs to each other or another group.

Play recordings of several different instruments. Try to recognize them by sound.

Create interviews for other careers in the arts not featured in the girls' book, such as weaver, museum director, set designer, puppeteer, art teacher, etc.

More "World of the Out-of-Doors" Activities

Plan a park for your neighborhood. Imagine you could put it any place you wanted. Decide on the kinds of jobs you would need to run your park.

Find work on a temporary or permanent basis, caring for an animal(s) or plant(s). Keep a record of the different tasks you need to remember to do on your job.

Make up a puppet show or dramatization of one of these titles:

- The Day I Cared for a Gorilla
- A Week in the Life of a Beekeeper
- My Weekend Working at the Animal Shelter
- Tricks to Teach a Dog
- Ways to Win and Keep an Anteater Happy
- Peanut Shells, Paper, and Popcorn, or a Day in the Life of the Zoo's Cleanup Crew

Visit a florist shop, nursery, garden center, botanical garden, garden club, or Christmas tree farm to find out about jobs for plant lovers.

Inquire about jobs near you that involve working on the water.

Look for people who work on oceans, rivers, canals, lakes, bays, at the waterfront, and on the sea.

Design a poster to promote protection of endangered species.

Set up an environmental information booth in a public place.

Conduct walking tours of your area, pointing out the natural resources.

Observe an animal or plant in different seasons. Carefully record the changes you see.

Interview people you see at work in the world of the out-of-doors. Photograph them at work.

Visit the library and find books about early pioneers and their way of life. Practice some of the early ways of doing things on your next camping trip.

Help others learn about the wildlife in your area by setting up a display.

Bibliography

Books for Leaders

Bureau of Labor Statistics, U.S. Department of Labor. *Occupational Outlook Handbook, 1976–77 Edition.* Washington, D.C.: U.S. Government Printing Office, 1976.

> The results of a voluminous study of career outlooks for the future, job qualifications required or recommended, and instructions for ordering Bureau publications. Includes a complete "Dictionary of Occupational Titles."

Career Bibliography: A Guide to Free and Inexpensive Occupational Information. University Park, Pa.: Career Development and Placement Center, The Pennsylvania State University, 1977.

> Compilation of titles of over 5,000 pamphlets about 522 occupations, with addresses where they may be obtained. Includes index of occupational titles grouped in appropriate job clusters.

Hoyt, Kenneth B. et al. *Career Education: What It Is and How to Do It.* (Second Edition) Salt Lake City: Olympus Publishing Co., 1974.

> Presents key concepts of career education, arguing persuasively the need for it and describing existing methods of implementation.

McClure, Larry. *Career Education Survival Manual: A Guidebook for Career Educators and Their Friends.* Salt Lake City: Olympus Publishing Co., 1975.

> General overview of career education attitudes and concepts and a review of past and current programs, structured in an index format and offering an extensive bibliography.

Books for Both Leaders and Girls

Adventures in the World of Work series. New York: Random House, 1976. (Fifth Grade and Up)

> Series of paperbacks focusing on careers in 12 general fields of work, with descriptions of challenges and rewards in specific careers, as narrated by people in those careers, and containing resource guides for additional information about each career cluster. Titles include:

Who Puts the Light in the Light Bulb?
Who Puts the Print on the Page?
Who Puts the Ice in the Cream?
Who Puts the Blue in the Jeans?
Who Puts the Plane in the Air?
Who Puts the Fun in Free Time?
Who Puts the Room in the House?
Who Puts the Grooves in the Record?
Who Puts the News on Television?
Who Puts the Care in Health Care?
Who Keeps American Clean?
Who Works for You?

Fiarotta, Phyllis, and Fiarotta, Noel. *Be What You Want to Be.* New York: Workman Publishing Co., 1977. (Kindergarten through 7th Grade)

Introduces craft ideas to help children role play more than 35 professions and occupations, using materials readily available in the home and presenting step-by-step instructions in large print, attractive illustrations, and close-up photographs.

Real People at Work series. Cleveland: Changing Times Education Service, Educational Research Council of America, 1976.

Series of 150 paperback booklets depicting females in a wide variety of careers in 15 different reading levels from low second grade to high sixth grade, each featuring a case study of one or more real people on the job.

Careers: Working with Animals. Washington, D.C.: The Humane Society of the United States, 1974.

Student Edition describes careers in veterinary medicine, zoos, parks, and education, and furnishes a lengthy compilation of sources for information and of schools offering career preparation programs.